This book belongs to

_____

Our Ancestories

IDIA
of the Benin Kingdom

Written by Ekiuwa Aire

Illustrated by Alina Shabelnyk

ISBN: 978-1-7771179-1-7 (Electronic)
978-1-7771179-0-0 (Hardcover)

Front cover image by Alina Shabelnyk.

Book design by Praise Saflor.

First printing edition 2020.

www.our-ancestories.com

To my loving husband, Meata, who has been so supportive throughout this process and has always encouraged me to pursue my passions.

To my darling daughters, Aize and Ivie, whom I love exceedingly and who inspired me to write this book.

Ekiuwa Aire

In the African kingdom of Benin, a young girl named Idia was sleeping. She tossed and turned, her mind full of strange images. In her dream, a woman was fighting in a raging battle. Arrows zipped through the air at her from all directions, but they missed. Her magic charms protected her.

Quickly, the dream changed: the battle was over, and the brave woman helped to heal those who were hurt by mixing herbs and potions and making the wounded fighters feel better with a single touch.

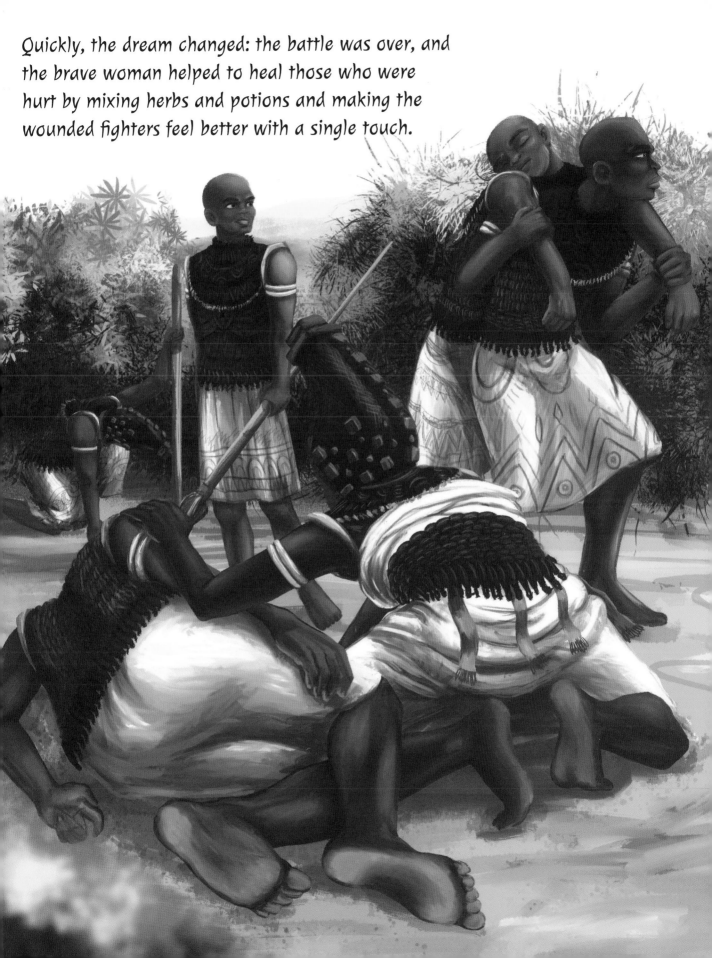

Idia woke up with a start. What a strange dream, she thought as she dressed hurriedly.

She had always been fascinated with tales of heroic battles and with magic. But such things did not happen here. The kingdom was peaceful, admired by visitors from all over the world, and its people were happy.

Idia's thoughts returned to the dream. Who was that woman? Women do not go to war. What could the dream mean?

Idia said good morning to her parents and then ran outside to meet her friend, Adesuwa.

"Let's hurry," Idia said. "I want to get there early!"

Today was the Igue festival. A day of celebration in the village of Ugieghudu.

There would be food, music, and dancing. Idia couldn't wait!

Up the wide, dusty trail, Idia and her friend
went, skipping and laughing all the way.

"Slow down! You'll wear yourself out before we
get there," warned Adesuwa.

"Can you do this?" Idia asked, rolling her arms
and shoulders. She cleverly drummed her feet to
the familiar rhythm of the *ema* (drum).

Idia made it look like such fun that soon
Adesuwa danced along the path too.

People buzzed with excitement in the centre of the village. The *Oba* (king) was there. Hands slapped drums. Fires were started to cook the feast. Idia adjusted her beads and greeted all her friends.

The young villagers had learned a
special dance for the occasion.

Idia performed as though she had been
born dancing! She held her head high
as her arms and legs moved in perfect
time to the rhythm. People clapped,
and her parents beamed with pride.

"You dance beautifully," Idia's father told her afterwards. Idia smiled, happy that her father had noticed how she danced.

But the dream was still on Idia's mind. She couldn't get it out of her head. Maybe she should talk to her father about it. He was a village elder and a warrior.

"*Erha* (Father)," she said. "Tell me, what is it like to be a warrior?"

Her father was a wise man. "It is hard work," he said, "and a big responsibility."

"But what is it like?" Idia persisted. "Why must we have war? What is the meaning of the warriors' secret ceremonies? Are you afraid when you fight?"

"So many questions!" said Idia's father. "You will not need to be a warrior, *uvbi* (little girl). You should spend your time having fun dancing."

However, the dream would not let her rest. "Maybe I can't be a warrior," she said, "but can I learn some of the things that a warrior learns?"

Her father sighed when he saw that his daughter would not give up. "If you agree to keep practising your dancing," he said, "I will talk to you every night about being a warrior."

"Thank you," cried Idia, delighted.

Every day, Idia danced. The more she danced, the better she became. The better she became, the more her father taught her about what it meant to be a warrior.

He taught her about battle plans, and how to deal with an enemy, and he even let her handle his weapons. Idia remembered all that she was taught, and she also remembered her dream.

One day, Idia was helping her mother fetch water.
Her mom stopped to gather plants.

"*Iye* (Mother), please tell me," she said, "about plants and healing, magic and medicine." Idia's mother knew a lot about these arts.

"You're much too young to worry about these things," said her mother.

"Please, I want to know," Idia kept asking.
Her dream still lingered in her memory.

Her mother finally gave in. "You really want to learn about these things?"

Idia nodded, proud and sure of herself.

"Very well, then," her mother agreed. "Perform your chores properly each day, and I will teach you about medicine and magic."

From that day, whatever her mother asked her to do, Idia did. In return, her mother taught her about the gods and about medicine.

Many years later, when Idia was older, she was invited to perform another dance with the village's best dancers for the young new Oba. The Oba enjoyed watching the dance. He also noticed Idia's energy, confidence, and rhythm.

Later, the Oba sent messengers to Idia's home. He wanted to marry her. Idia was quiet for days afterwards. It would be unwise to refuse the Oba, but she didn't know if marrying him was the right thing to do.

To help them with their decision, Idia's parents summoned a native doctor.

He chanted special prayers for protection and wisdom for Idia.

He also made two deep marks in Idia's forehead, to which he applied special medicines.

After the ceremony, Idia fell into a deep sleep.

She began to dream. It was the same dream that she had as a child, but now that she was older, she could understand it clearly.

She was the woman in the dream. She was a queen, and her young son was a king. There were many bad people who were his enemies, and they brought war to his kingdom.

When Idia woke, she knew she must marry the Oba. Thanks to her dad, she knew everything she needed to know about ruling a kingdom. She was also very good with medicine and magic, thanks to her mother. The Kingdom of Benin would need her.

Rising, Idia rushed to her parents and told them about her dreams.

"*Osanobua* (God) has given you these dreams to show you your path," said her mother.

"You have always followed your heart, and you must do so now," said her father. "Your *ehi* (guardian angel) has determined your destiny. Your heart will lead you to where you are meant to be."

When the day came for Idia to be married, her parents hugged her tightly.

"Go bravely," said her father, "with joy and happiness. And promise me that, as you become a wife, mother, and warrior, you will not forget to dance."

"I will never forget," answered Idia. "And I will never forget you and Mother. I will be a strong, dancing, warrior queen, and make you both proud."

And that is just what she did. She became a queen, a warrior, the first woman to fight for the kingdom, and the

first Iyoba (Queen Mother) of Benin.

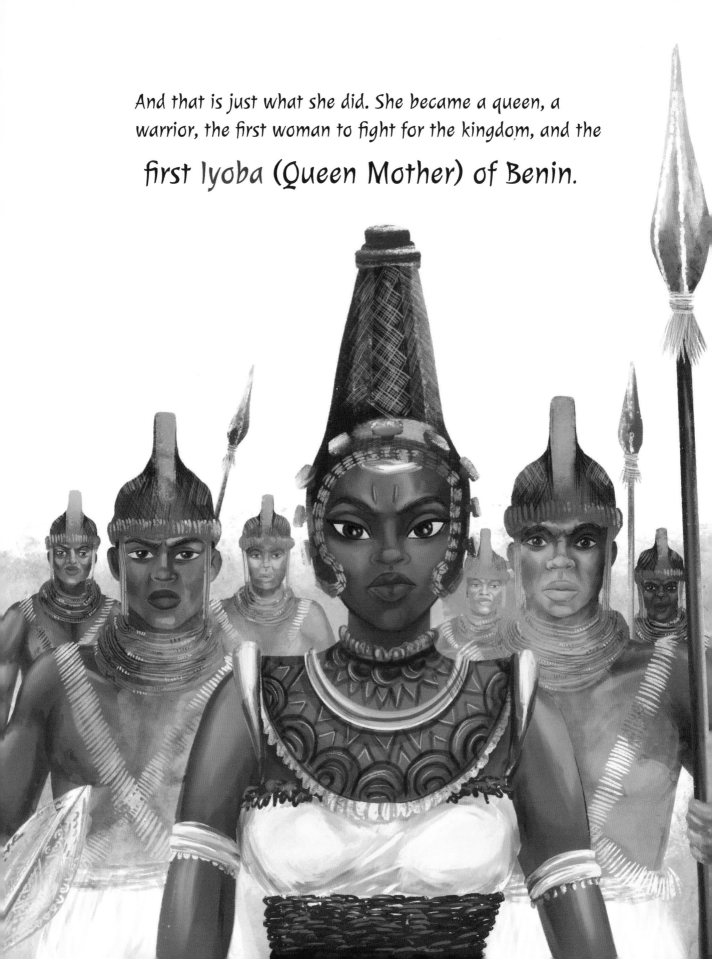

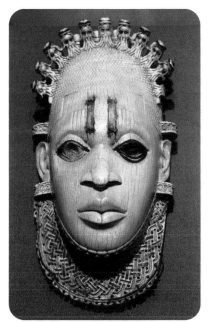

Ivory Mask of Idia—
British Museum, London

Queen Idia

was the mother of Esigie, the Oba (king) of Benin, who ruled from 1504 to 1550. She played a significant role in Esigie's rise and reign and is remembered as a great warrior who fought without fear before *and* during his reign as the Oba of the Edo people.

As a patron of the arts, Iyoba Idia was responsible for many innovations (such as the Ekassa dance) that still hold firm in Benin's cultural history to date. The famous Idah Battle of 1515 couldn't have been won if it weren't for Iyoba Idia's clever plan, which was to dress up as a man and march alongside her son to win the war for him. She protected Esigie with her life and cunningly avoided many assassination attempts to save him.

After her death, Oba Esigie ordered his craftsmen to build bronze heads and masks of his mother to honor her military achievements and ceremonial power. These works of art were placed either in front of altars or inside Idia's palace. They were also part of an exclusive collection of wealth belonging to the Oba of Benin. Some of these were taken by the British during the invasive Expedition of 1897.

Today, the Bronze Head of Queen Idia can be found in the British Museum, the World Museum in Liverpool, the Nigerian National Museum in Lagos, and the Ethnological Museum of Berlin.

The Benin Ivory Mask of Queen Idia can be found at the British Museum in London, the Metropolitan Museum of Art in New York City, the Seattle Art Museum, and the Linden Museum. The Ivory Mask is among the Metropolitan Museum of Art (also known as 'the Met')'s most celebrated works. This mask (and pictures thereof), believed to be a true likeness of Queen Iyoba Idia, has become a mascot and souvenir in her honor, and can be found on different memorabilia like trays, cups, plates, and cloth, and on jewelry and plaques made from ebony or brass.

Bronze Head of Idia—
Ethnological Museum of Berlin

Queen Idia left a legacy of strength, delicacy, and musical rhythm within the Benin kingdom. And for this, she will always be admired and highly respected. Today, the Oba of Benin still leads religious ceremonies, but no longer rules over his people.

The Edo people were the original residents of the Benin Empire. The Ogiso (Kings of the Sky) Dynasty were their first rulers. They called their land 'Igodomigodo'. When the Ogiso Dynasty ended in 1100 CE, the Oba Dynasty took over as the new rulers.

The Benin Empire was one of the more advanced kingdoms in West Africa. Its city (Benin City) was planned following the careful rules of symmetry, proportionality, and repetition, now known as 'Fractal Design'.

For over four hundred years, a series of trenches made up of banks and ditches called 'Iya' protected the kingdom. These human-made marvels are popularly referred to as the walls of Benin City. Some parts of the walls are still standing to this day.

In 1897, British troops burned the original Benin City to the ground. This invasion led to the Kingdom of Benin becoming part of the British Empire until 1960. After that, it formed part of the independent country of Nigeria and is still a part of Nigeria today.

Map of Benin

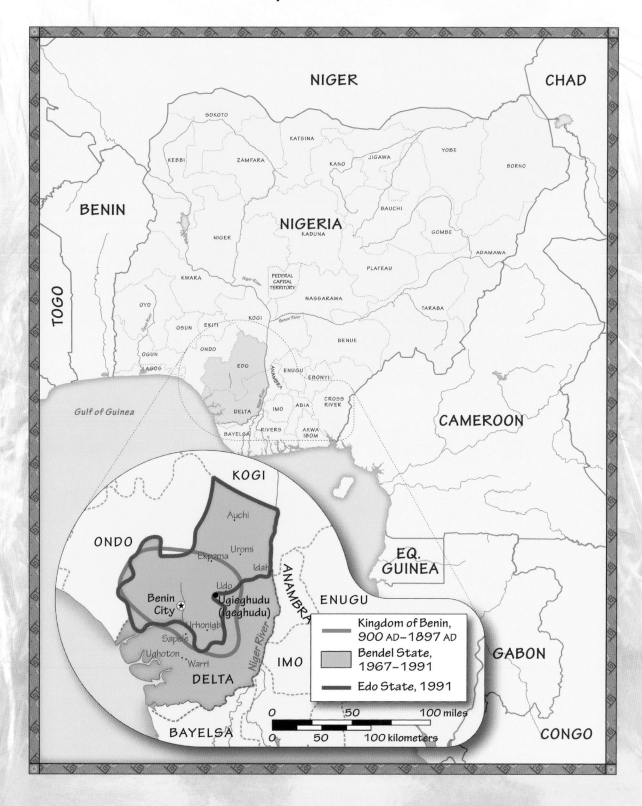

About the Author

Ekiuwa Aire was born and raised in Benin City, Edo, Nigeria. Ekiuwa's passion for African history emerged when she left Nigeria for Canada in 2007. When she became a mother, Ekiuwa realized that there were not a lot of resources to introduce African history to her young children. She wanted her kids (and other kids) to understand the heritage of this history and to value the wisdom and pride that came from this knowledge. This desire spurred her to write her first picture book about Queen Idia, Idia of the Benin Kingdom.

About the Illustrator

Alina Shabelnyk is an illustrator from Ukraine. She really loves to draw—everywhere, and all the time. When she was a child, Alina dreamed of illustrating children's books, and she realized that dream was meant to be her life's work when she saw children happily leafing through a book that she illustrated. She is very inspired to think that thousands of children around the world enjoy her illustrations every day. Alina believes that these books help children find self-confidence and overcome their fears.

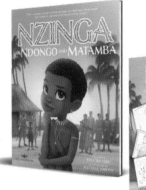

Printed in Great Britain
by Amazon